ISBN: 978-0-615-50699-9

DEDICATION

This book of short stories is dedicated to my parents
Mr. Sabry Abdel-Aziz and Mrs. Azima Hamad Abdel-Aziz who
worked very hard to instill in my twin sister, Samar, and I love for
Islam, even when there were few Muslims around.

THANKS TO

My husband Dr. Hani Soliman
My children Ms. Hadeer, Mr. Siraj and Ms. Janna Soliman
New Horizon School Los Angeles principal, staff and students
Islamic Center of Irvine Summer Camp members and parents

All proceeds will go to an
Islamic educational institution.

Table of Contents

Preface

In 1998 when Christmas, Hanukkah, and Ramadan were all celebrated during the month of December, I took my three children, 9-year-old Hadeer, 8-year-old Siraj, and 6-year-old Janna, to Story Time at the local library. With great excitement, the librarian told the wide-eyed children that she would read stories about the holidays in December to them: Christmas and Hanukkah. My daughter Hadeer, almost automatically, said to me, "How about Ramadan, Mommy? That's in December too." After Story Time was over I asked the librarian to share with the children a story about Ramadan too because all three holidays coincided this year. The librarian retorted, "Ramadan is not a fun month; it's a religious holiday."

I proceeded to tell her that like Christmas and Hanukkah, Ramadan is also a religious time and that it is, in fact, fun, just like those two holidays. After a long discussion on this matter the librarian agreed. If I could bring her a children's story about Ramadan she would share it during Story Time at the library. Naturally, I looked in the library for a children's short story about Ramadan. However, to my children's disappointment, and mine, there were none.

That is when I began working with my children on building off of their own experiences to write a story about Ramadan. I also designed an art project for the children to participate in during Story Time the following week at the library. Elhamdulilah, the following week we were ready with a story to share with the children and we made a lantern as the library's art project for the week.

The following year, when I started teaching and developing the Islamic Studies curriculum at New Horizon School in Los Angeles, CA, I asked my students to write short stories about Ramadan. I also requested that they write poems about the Quran, Ramadan, Eid, the Prophet Mohammad (pbuh), and thankfulness. I then worked on developing creative ideas for art projects to bring to life Islamic ideas and help us celebrate Islamic holidays.

Not only did we adapt existing arts and crafts projects already out there to relate them to Islam, we also created brand new ideas and taught the students to relate everything we used to the One who created the materials: God. We taught them that all man-made items are from God's natural creations, such as wax. We asked the students what wax is made of and encouraged them do their research, and come back to class with an answer. "Wax is made from natural things like cattle fat, sugars, and honey," they wrote. Then we asked them what people use wax for. "People use wax for things like crayons, candles, and cosmetics," they'd answer. We wanted to clarify to the students that using their creativity and God's creation, you could produce beautiful art!

I hope my story will encourage other parents to work with their local communities and inspire their children to be proud of and to use their resources to develop their Muslim American identities.

Sahar Sabry Abdel-Aziz

Arabic Words

What is Ramadan ?

Ramadan is the ninth month in the Islamic calendar. During this month Muslims all over the world fast (refrain from eating, drinking, and more) from sunrise to sunset. Fasting is meant to teach the Muslim patience, modesty, and spirituality. Ramadan is considered the holiest month of the year in Islam. It is a time when Muslims offer more prayers than usual, ask for more forgiveness from Allah for past sins, pray for more guidance and help in refraining from everyday harms and try to purify themselves through self-discipline and good deeds.

Allah	God
Asr	The third prayer of the day
Assalamu Alaikum	Peace be upon you
Bismillah	In the name of God
Duaa	Making a supplication to God
Duhr	The second prayer of the day
Eid	Holiday
Elhamdulilah	Thank God
Fajr	First prayer of the day
Hajj	Pilgrimage made once in life by every able Muslim
Hijab	Head scarf
Iftar	First meal after breaking the fast
InshaAllah	God willing
Isha	Last prayer of the day
Maghrib	The fourth prayer of the day
Masjid	Place where Muslims go to pray/Mosque
Mubarak	Blessed
Quran	The holy book of Islam
Sadaka	Charity given to the poor at anytime
Saed	Happy
Shaaban	Islamic month before Ramadan
Suhur	A meal eaten before sunrise
Taraweeh	An extra prayer during the month of Ramadan
Ul Fitr	The Islamic holiday the day after Ramadan ends

1
Fatima's First Day of Fasting

Written By:
Hadeer Soliman

Illustrated By:
Hadeer Soliman &
Engie Salama
New Horizon School
LA

One night Fatima was looking at the sky. She got up on a hill then she saw the. . . the. . . It was the moon! "A crescent!" she said. Then she ran home and asked her mom where the calendar was.

"It's near the dining table," her mother said. Fatima found it and checked to see when Ramadan was coming. "It is today. The first day of Ramadan is today!" Fatima said.

She thought about how exciting it would be. Then she remembered that she was 10 years old and that she had to fast the whole month of Ramadan.

But she didn't know it was today! Her mother did not even wake her up for Suhur.

Later, she lay on her bed thinking about Ramadan until she fell asleep. She dreamt that she had missed fasting this Ramadan.   Then suddenly someone tapped Fatima on the shoulders. It was her sister Aisha. "Wake up," she said, "Come to dinner. We are all waiting for you."

She came to the table. Nobody talked about Ramadan. They just talked about Aisha's school grades. Then when they stopped talking for a while, Fatima said, "I checked the calendar and it said that today is Ramadan. How come no one cares?"

"Show me this calendar!" her dad said. Fatima got up and brought the calendar to the table. "Here it is," Fatima said. "This is the calendar?" Fatima's dad laughed.

"This is next year's calendar, not this year's. Ramadan comes 11 days earlier every year. We still have 11 more days until Ramadan!" "Where is this year's calendar, Mama?" Fatima asked.

"It is in the drawer," Mama answered. When she brought it to the table Fatima looked at the calendar happily. "Wow! We still have 11 days before Ramadan!" Fatima exclaimed. "Elhamdulilah! I feel so relieved." Eleven days passed by so quickly. Every day Fatima checked the calendar. Then the big day came!

Fatima woke up at 3 o'clock in the morning and woke everyone else up at 4 o'clock.

Her family found food on the table for Suhur. Fatima had prepared it for everyone.

They all said the Duaa and ate before they prayed Fajr. At 7 o'clock Aisha went to school, her dad went to work and Fatima read the Quran with her mother.

At 8 o'clock Fatima got ready for school.

In the car on her way to school she said her Quran memorization and her Duaa.

She fasted the whole day in school even though they had a bake sale that day.

Fatima had to keep reminding herself that she was fasting.

13

At 3 o'clock Fatima went home
and rested for an hour.

When Aisha came home they talked
about the first day of fasting, read the
Quran together and did some of their
homework.

They all broke their fast by saying the
Duaa and eating dates like the Prophet
Mohammed (peace be upon him) used to
do. Then they prayed Maghrib and
started to eat the Iftar meal.

After the meal, they prayed
Isha and Taraweeh.

They did this for 30 days until Ramadan was over. But the last day was different.

After the last Iftar meal everyone got new clothes and presents for Eid Ul Fitr.

Eid Ul Fitr is the end of Ramadan. It is a feast, the celebration of breaking the fast.

On this day Muslims give their Zakat to the poor.

This has to be done before the Eid Ul Fitr prayer so Allah will accept their fasting. They also give Sadaka at other times.

Even though her father was taking care of the Zakat for her, she wanted to give Zakat from her own money too.

Fatima was so happy she fasted. Aisha was also very glad her sister Fatima fasted. Fatima's family gave her presents.

This was the most joyous time of her life.

2
The Boy Who Couldn't Fast But Tried

Once there were two brothers named Adam and Sameer. Sameer was seven years old and Adam was 12 years old. Whenever Adam fasted he got dizzy and wanted to drink something, so he never fasted.

Sameer would fast, but missed some days. But that was still good.

Everyday when Adam and Sameer would go to school, Adam's friends would tease him by saying, "You don't fast, but Sameer does, I think he's better than you."

Or, "I can't believe you're 12 years old, and Sameer is only seven. How come Sameer can fast, but you can't?"

Adam always got mad at his friends and was embarrassed. They were saying those things in front of everybody and they all laughed at him. When they got home, Sameer told Adam that he should try to fast and Adam said, "How can I fast? I always get dizzy, hungry and thirsty."

Sameer said, "Just keep on trying." So the following day, Adam kept his fast and he went to school, but he got so dizzy and sick he had to break his fast at mid-day.

All the children laughed at him.

He was so embarrassed that he went home.

But Adam kept trying and trying. On Saturday, he finally kept his fast and he was so happy. His friends stopped teasing him and apologized to him because you shouldn't tease someone who is trying their best. Adam was never embarrassed again. He fasted many times after that.

From that day on, Adam kept fasting during Ramadan and everyone was proud of him, including Sameer.

3
<u>In This</u>
<u>Ramadan</u>

Once there was a girl named Manisha. She wanted to fast this year so she went to her mom and said, "Can I fast this year?" "Not the whole month, but you can fast some days," her mother said. The next day was the first Friday of Ramadan and her mom said that she could fast. She was really happy. Manisha said, "Thank you, mother, thank you."

"Thank you for reminding me. If you didn't remind me, I would have eaten the whole plate!" Manisha said.

4
The
Children
Who Fasted

Once there were two Muslim children named Ahmad and Mary. They lived in a city with many Muslim children and lots of mosques. They were so excited because Ramadan was coming so they went to sleep early for Suhur. Before they slept they packed everything for school the next day.

The next day they woke up for Suhur and stayed awake after that to correct their homework and get ready for school. By the time it was 6 o'clock their parents had to rush. Ahmad and Mary laughed because their parents were running around and forgetting where they put their things.

Finally, their father dropped them off at school. Mary greeted her friends and so did Ahmad. Mary walked off to class with her friend Lily. Ahmad walked with Ibrahim to class.

At school, they worked hard to take their mind off of food. When the bell rang, everyone got in line and waited for the teacher to tell them to go to recess.

Mary told Ahmad not to play too hard because he would get tired and thirsty. But Ahmad didn't listen.

He said, "No, I won't!"

After recess everyone went back to class. The class had a three-minute break to rest, drink water and do anything else they needed to do. Ahmad was really thirsty and remembered what his sister told him at recess. Ahmad wished that he had listened to her.

At lunch the children who were not fasting got their lunches and lined up to go to the cafeteria. Ahmad and Mary did not go to the cafeteria because they were fasting. They did not want to be in a place where people were eating.

The teacher knew they were fasting so she let them go play outside. Mary just wanted to sit down and read. Ahmad remembered what Mary said at recess so he just tried to throw basketballs into the hoop.

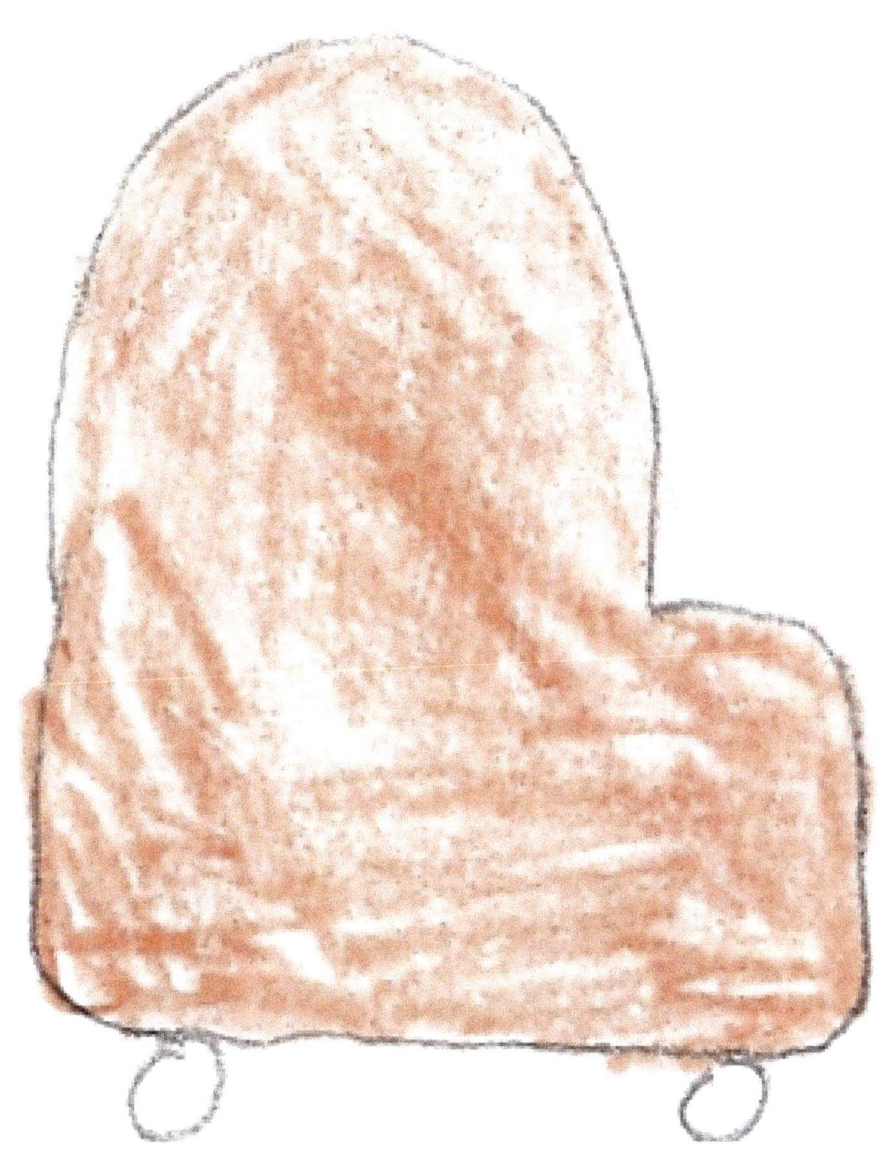

Finally their mother picked them up from school. Ahmad and Mary were so excited that they could go home. They were excited because it was almost time to break the fast so they could eat.

At home their mother began cooking dinner. The children took a shower, got dressed and set the table. At 7:30 p.m. their father came home from work and got ready for Iftar. Then they broke their fast and prayed Maghrib.

After prayer everyone ate a lot, but did not overeat. When everyone was finished eating they had a small break before they had another course of homemade cookies and tea. Ahmad and Mary drank hot chocolate.

After dinner Mary watched television and Ahmad finished his crossword puzzle book. Their dad was reading the newspaper and their mom was reading the Quran.

At night everyone went to sleep and the house was so peaceful and quiet.

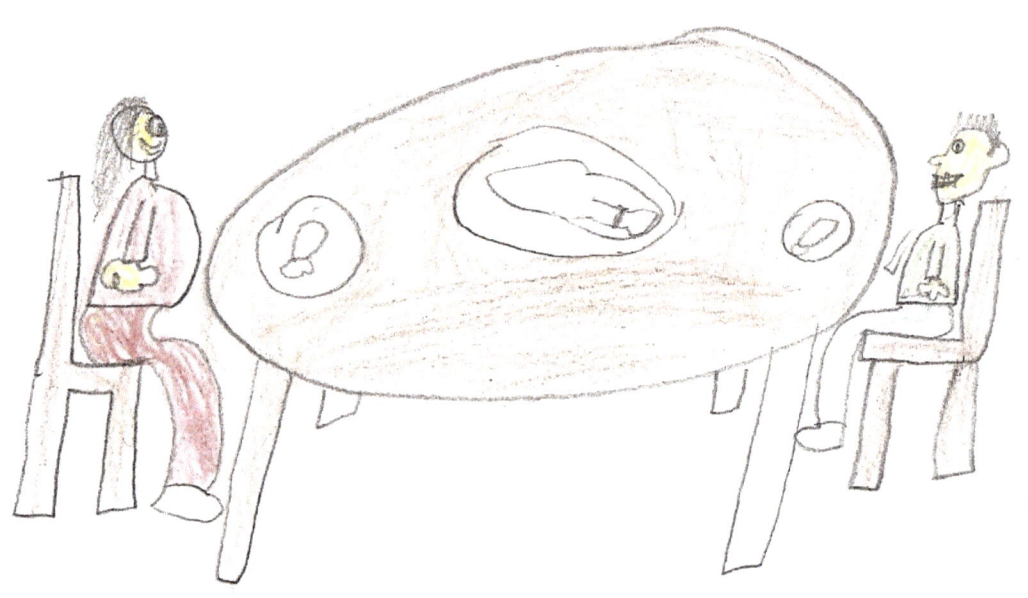

5

<u>Adam's</u>
<u>Exciting Wait</u>
<u>for Ramadan</u>

There was once a boy named Adam and he lived with his parents and little sister. His parent's names were Muhammad and Khadija and his little sister's name was Yasmine.

One day Adam got up and brushed his teeth, changed into his uniform and went to school. When he got to school he met his friends Ahmed, Bahia, Fatima and Hassan. Their first class was art.

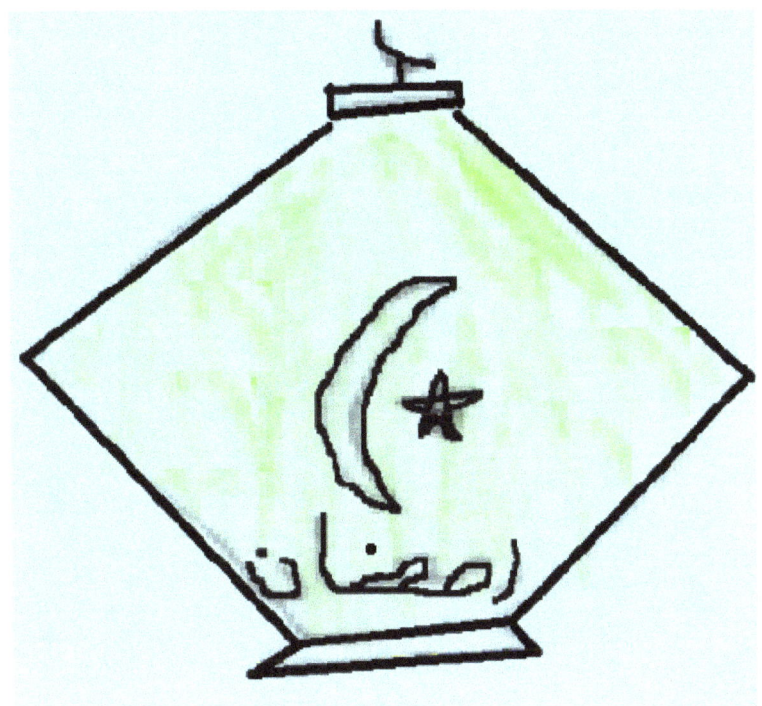

They made lanterns for Ramadan. Then during lunch they talked about how much fun Ramadan would be. After school they went to the mosque to pray Asr. And then they went home.

When they got home they all ate dinner with their parents, prayed Maghrib then did their homework.

At 7:00 p.m. Adam took a bath, made Wudu and then prayed Isha. After Isha he watched cartoons with his sister Yasmine. Then at 8:00 p.m. he went to bed.

The next day, Adam and his dad went with his friends down the street to buy a loaf of bread and milk. When they got back, he saw his grandparents and greeted them Ramadan Mubarak.

After that they ate dinner, prayed Maghrib and then they read the Quran until it was time for Isha. And that is how Adam's Ramadan began!

6
My Friend Who Fasted

One day in Ramadan we went to someone's house for Iftar. The ride was long and it took us quite some time to get to the house. The sun went down before we got there so we had to break our fast in the car.

Finally, we arrived at the house. We went inside and ate some food and I played with my friend. My friend told me she didn't fast. I said, "You have to fast!"

"It's too hard. I have to eat
something!" she said.

"You have to try like everyone else," I said.

The next day we went to their house again, but this time my friend was fasting.
She said she tried her best. She was about to give up, but she didn't.

When it was time to break the fast, she ate a lot of food and then prayed with us.

I fasted day after day until a day before Eid. The day of Eid I had to wear nice clothes to go to the Masjid and then to my friend's house to celebrate. I was really happy because my friend had fasted in Ramadan. Everyone was proud of her and of me because I encouraged her to fast.

The next Ramadan my friend fasted every day. She even made up her sick days. I was really proud of my friend.

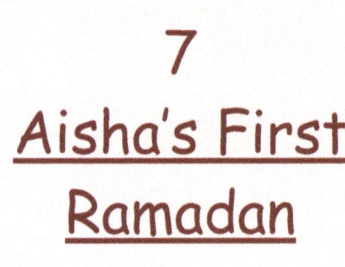

7
Aisha's First Ramadan

Written By:
Nabeeha Aleem
New Horizon School LA

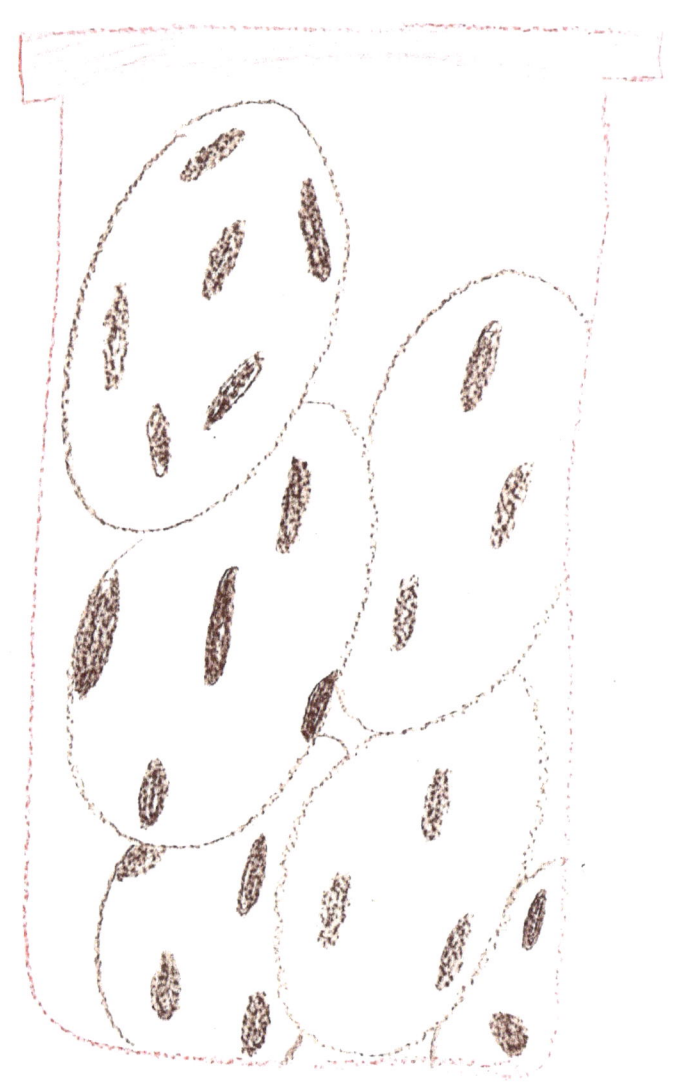

There was once was a girl named Aisha. She told her mother that she wanted to fast during Ramadan. So the next day her mom woke her up for Suhur. Aisha ate her Suhur and prayed Fajr then went back to sleep. A little while later, her mom woke her up for school.

At lunchtime, when Aisha saw the boys and girls eating food, she felt hungry. When she got home she felt dizzy. Soon it was Iftar time and Aisha felt better when she ate all the good food. After Iftar she prayed Maghrib with her family.

The next day, since it was Saturday, Aisha woke up at lunchtime and saw some yummy treats.

She almost took a bite out of a cookie before she remembered that she was fasting.

"Aisha put the cookie down," she thought.

When it was Iftar time she ate and then she prayed Maghrib.

37

The next morning she felt sick but she still wanted to fast. Her mother said, "You might get sicker." Aisha didn't want that to happen so she didn't fast. She rested the whole day.

When she woke up the next day she was better so she fasted after Suhur. She prayed Fajr, read the Quran and went to sleep. Aisha went to school but she had a stomachache and was dizzy. So she broke her fast and took some medicine.

The next few days were the last days of Ramadan. Aisha still had a stomachache and felt dizzy. The doctor told her not to fast.

Then Ramadan ended. Aisha said that she will have to make up the days after Ramadan InshaAllah and try to fast again next year.

But she got a gift from her parents for all her effort.

8
Ahmed's
Birthday

Ahmed's birthday was on the first day of Ramadan and he wanted to fast. But his mom thought he was too young. So Ahmed said, "If you let me fast for one day, I will clean the house for one week!"

That sounded good to his mom, so it was official that Ahmed was going to fast on the first day of Ramadan. When it was the night before Ramadan Ahmed was so excited that he didn't go to sleep until past midnight. When it was finally Ramadan he ate Suhur and prayed Fajr prayer.

When Ahmed left his house he met his friends who were also fasting. Then he saw small children eating food so he ran to the park to play soccer to keep him from seeing food everywhere.

After one hour, Ahmed sat down to rest. He felt very hungry.

He saw some people eating his favorite chips, but he fought his temptations.

Ahmed ran as fast as he could, but everywhere he went he saw food. He ran to his friend's house, but since his friend was sick he was not fasting. He ran to his house and told his mom, "I can't take it anymore!"

Ahmed's mom said, "It is already time to break the fast!"

Ahmed was so happy that he gave his mom a big hug. He ate with his family during Iftar time and afterward they gave him gifts.

9
What Happened in Ramadan

Samantha where are you

One day a girl named Erum was at her friend Samantha's house. They played a few games then it was time for Erum to go home. Erum ate dinner with her family and then went to sleep early because the next day would be Ramadan.

Erum woke up the next morning, ate Suhur then prayed Fajr. Afterwards she got ready for school.

When Erum got to school a lot of people asked her, "Where is your lunch?" So she explained why she didn't have one.

When Erum got home, she asked Samantha to come over. When Samantha got there Erum was reading the Quran.

Samantha wondered what Erum was saying so Erum taught Samantha how to be a Muslim.

When Samantha got home she told her parents about Erum. Erum's family called Samantha's family to come over for Iftar the next day. When they got to Erum's house, they asked a lot of questions and learned a lot about Islam. Both families were very happy.

10
What We Do in Ramadan and Eid Ul Fitr

Written By:
Hadeer Soliman
New Horizon School LA

Khadija looked at the Islamic calendar. "Oh, wow! It was the last day of Shaaban, which means tomorrow is Ramadan!" she exclaimed.

She called all her friends and asked them what they would be doing during Ramadan.

Ramadan is the month when the Quran was sent to the Prophet Muhammed (peace be upon him) as guidance to mankind. Muslims read the Quran more often during Ramadan.

They do not eat or drink from sunrise to sunset. Fasting Muslims should also have good manners.

They should also pray an extra prayer called Taraweeh.

Khadija's friends said they would meet at the Masjid at 3:00 p.m. Khadija waited until 2:30 p.m. then she left her home. When she arrived at the Masjid, she found her friends Sarrah, Hanna, Samira, Janna and Fatima.

Everyday Khadija's family and friends would meet at the Masjid to read one part of the Quran, learn more about manners and behavior during fasting and then break their fast together.

They also prayed Maghrib together.

Khadija and her friends made their Ramadan lanterns and wished each other, "Ramadan Kareem!"

They also wished all the Muslims in the Masjid, "Ramadan Kareem!" and agreed to meet every night during Ramadan to pray Taraweeh.

They also agreed to fast the whole month of Ramadan.

The end of Ramadan is celebrated with a big holiday called Eid Ul Fitr. Khadija and her family and friends celebrated the Eid by going to the Masjid for prayers. Everyone wished each other, "Eid Saed!" "Eid Mubarak!" or "Happy Eid!"

They were all dressed up and went to the Masjid early in the morning for prayer. After the prayers the parents gave gifts to their children, wished them "Eid Mubarak" and congratulated them on their good behavior during Ramadan.

They hoped they would continue their good behavior all the time. All the children were happy because they fasted the whole month of Ramadan and behaved well.

After Eid prayer, Khadija, her friends and her family went to have breakfast. After breakfast, they all went to the park to play and have fun together.

11
Mohamed's Ramadan Fast

Written By:
Siraj Soliman

Illustrated By:
Siraj Soliman
& Hakim Kebir
New Horizon School LA

One day a boy named Mohamed was walking to school when he remembered that Ramadan was the next day. When he finished school, he ran to his mom and dad and said, "Ramadan is tomorrow!"

"Good job, you remembered!" his mom said. "Are you going to fast this year?" his father asked. "Yes!" Mohamed replied.

The next day Mohamed woke up for Suhur. He smelled a very good smell. He wondered what his mother was cooking.

He went down and asked, "Mom, what are you cooking?"

"Eggs, beans and soup for Suhur," she replied.

"Yum!" Mohamed said.

"I hope you like it!" His mom said and then smiled. Mohamed sat down at the table when the food was ready and his dad came right away.

Mohamed ate eggs and soup before he drank some milk. Now, it was 5 o'clock in the morning so he sat down and read the Quran. He read five pages, prayed Fajr and then got ready for school.

The next day at school everyone was fasting. His friend Ahmed said, "Let's go play ball!"

"No, I do not want to get sweaty and thirsty," Mohamed told his friend.

"You are right," agreed Ahmed.

It was soon Duhr prayer time so Ahmed said, "Let's pray Duhr."

They both went to pray. When they finished the prayer, Ahmed went with Mohamed to his house. When it was Iftar time Ahmed's parents came to Mohamed's house.

Everyone ate dates, prayed Maghrib and then started the Iftar. After they finished Iftar they prayed Isha and Taraweeh together.

Ahmed slept at Mohamed's house. They woke up for Suhur. They ate, read the Quran, prayed Fajr and then got ready to go to school.

Ahmed and Mohamed saw their teacher in the morning. Ahmed invited his teacher to his house and gave him the address and phone number. After school Ahmed and Mohamed ran to Ahmed's house and helped their moms get ready for the Iftar gathering. They were free because they did not have any homework. Ahmed called his friend Osamah to invite him to have Iftar with them too.

Osamah was the first to arrive to the Iftar gathering. They played video games for an hour. Then their teacher came.

Everyone ate chicken, soup, beef, cheese, eggs, onions and rice. After eating they played video games, hide and seek and tag. Everyone had fun. Then they had milk and cookies for dessert. After playing it was time for Isha prayer so they prayed Isha and Taraweeh. After praying they read one part of the Quran together. On this night, Mohamed slept at Ahmed's house.

The next day Ahmed and Mohamed went to school together.

They were very happy to be together for two days.

12
Who Wants to be a Fasting Muslim

Written & Illustrated By:
Hakim Kebir
New Horizon School LA

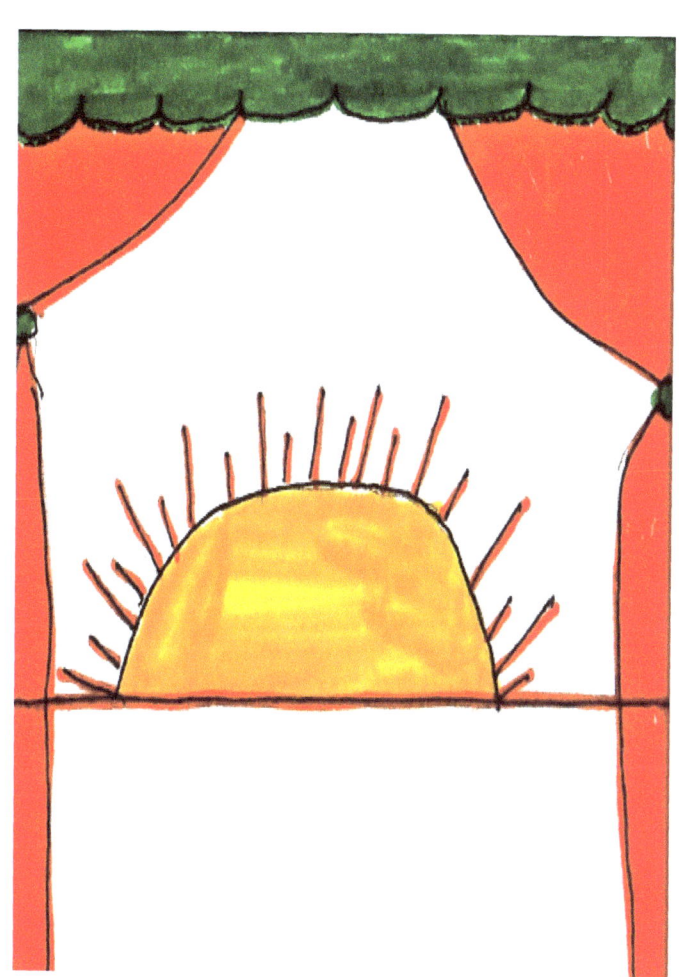

It was the night before Ramadan and everybody was ready for bed. "Don't forget to say your intention to fast in Ramadan," Mohammed's dad said.

"Okay," said Mohammed.

The next morning Mohammed woke up to get ready for Suhur, but the sun was already up. It was too late for Suhur so he went back to sleep.

When he finally got up he asked his mom for his breakfast.

His mom said, "You can still fast even though you didn't eat Suhur."

"Okay, I'll fast. Can I go to the park?" he said.

"That's fine," answered his dad. Mohammed got out his bike and sand toys then went to the park.

When he got home he read the Quran. After that he felt hungry and asked his dad, "Why do we fast?"

His dad said, "One reason is to know how the poor people feel everyday of their lives."

After talking to his dad Mohammed decided to go play with his friend Ahmed who was also trying to fast that day.

When he got home he smelled chocolate chip cookies fresh from the oven. He was so hungry that he put on a nose plug so he would not be tempted, but it didn't work.

He was too tempted that he forgot he was fasting and ate a delicious cookie and drank a glass of water.

He screamed, "Oh no! What have I done now?"

He ran to his mom and told her what had happened. She said, "Don't worry. It was a simple mistake. Allah will forgive you."

It was soon time for Iftar and Mohammed's mom said, "You did a good job so far!"

"I'm going to fast tomorrow, InshaAllah!" Mohammed said.

13
Ramadan

One day Alido got up late for Suhur. Alido asked his mom if he could still fast. "Yes, you can," she replied. "Hurray!" Alido jumped up and down because he was so happy. He prayed and then he helped his mom vacuum the house.

Later, the doorbell rang. It was his best friend Zeehasham. They watched television and played video games together.

Then Alido forgot he was fasting and he ate a cookie. He asked his mom, "Did I break my fast, Mama?"

"No, Alido. Just continue to fast," she said. Alido was so happy. Then Maghrib came. They ate Iftar, prayed and went to the mosque. They prayed Isha and Taraweeh there.

The next day Alido did not forget he was fasting. He went go carting with Zeehasham. They had so much fun, but they did not eat. They raced and raced. Alido and Zeehasham tied for many races.

And then Maghrib time came. They prayed then broke their fast by saying a special Duaa. They ate dates, drank milk and then they prayed.

They were so tired at the end day so they brushed their teeth and went to sleep.

14
The First Day of Ramadan

It was the first day of Ramadan. Madeeha and her family went to pray Taraweeh at the Masjid.

Then later, Madeeha's dad took her and her brother to see the moon. The moon was shaped like a crescent.

When they got back home Madeeha's mom asked her if she wanted to fast.

"Yes," Madeeha said. She wanted to know what it felt like to be without food or water from dawn until sunset.

The next day in the morning Madeeha's mom woke her up for Suhur.

She got up, washed her face and sat next to her brother at the table. They had cereal and milk. Madeeha asked her parents, "Why do we fast?"

"We fast to have self-discipline and to feel how the poor feel when they do not have food and, of course, because God told us to," her mom said.

After Suhur, Madeeha slept until noon.

When she got up, she went out to play with her friends and told them she was fasting.

When they asked her why she was fasting, she explained that she was learning self-discipline and how it feels to be poor and not have food.

When it was time for Iftar, Madeeha's mom called her to come and sit down. There was lots of food on the table that she liked to eat. She was hungry and ate a lot. After Iftar her dad asked her what she had learned from fasting. Madeeha said, "I am grateful to God that he provides us with food."

Madeeha's family prayed Maghrib then later her brother came to tell her they were going to pray Taraweeh. She put on her scarf and went downstairs to join her family. After Taraweeh they all went out for ice cream.

15
__Ramadan__
2000

My family fasted for all of Ramadan. Most of the nights we went to the mosque for Taraweeh prayer. Sometimes the mosque was very crowded.

There was childcare at the mosque, so one night I stayed outside to play basketball with my friends. Meanwhile, my mom and my brother were inside the mosque praying Taraweeh.

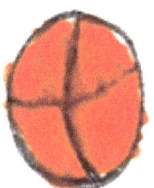

There were six of us. We played all night. Our team won the game.

Then one day we were invited for Iftar at my cousin's house.

Other friends of ours were invited too. There was a lot of food and many different kinds. The food was very delicious.

I ate so much that my stomach hurt a little.

Then a few days before Eid our cousin from Sweden came to visit us here in Los Angeles. That day my brother and I went to the airport to pick him up. I saw lots of airplanes landing and taking off. Also, I saw a nice big restaurant.

Then on Eid morning, my family and I went to Eid prayer. That morning, it was a little cold, but it was nice.

There was a good feeling in the air. When we arrived there, there were lots of cars and people.

After the prayer, people said, "Eid Mubarak!" to each other.

16
<u>Ramadan Story</u>

There was an 8-year-old girl named Amina. Her family was very excited because the next day was the first day of Ramadan.   When her grandfather Abdullah saw her, he asked, "Are you going to fast tomorrow?" "What's so special about tomorrow?" Amina answered his question with another question. "You don't know?" he replied. "Tomorrow is Ramadan. We fast from sunrise to sunset."

"Really?" Amina was surprised.

"Go ask your sister Jihad," Grandfather Abdullah suggested.

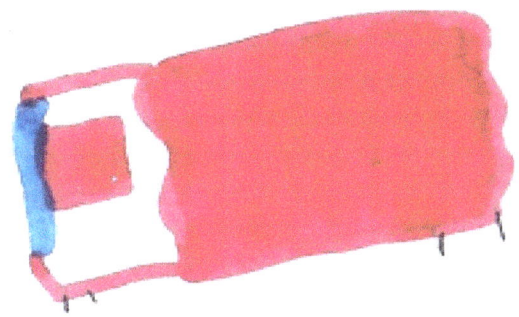

Amina went to Jihad's room and asked, "What's so special about tomorrow?" Jihad was surprised.

"You don't know?" she replied. "Tomorrow is Ramadan."

Amina already knew that, but she wanted to know what was so special about Ramadan. The answer didn't satisfy her so she asked, "What's Ramadan?"

"Ramadan is the month of fasting. Fasting means not eating or drinking from sunrise to sunset," Jihad explained patiently. "Won't we get hungry?" Amina felt hungry just thinking about it.

"We eat early in the morning before dawn. That's called Suhur," Jihad continued. "But why do we fast?" Amina's curiosity was not satisfied. "We fast so we can think about the poor. We should feel the way the poor feel with no food," Jihad reached for Amina's hands and smiled.

"One more question," Amina asked, "Did you fast last year?"
"Yes, I did," Jihad replied.

"Why didn't you tell me? Why didn't I fast too?" Amina wanted to know.

"You were too young," Jihad answered.

Amina's curiosity was satisfied. She felt happy because she knew the meaning of Ramadan. She went into the kitchen and saw her parents at the table.

"May I fast tomorrow?" she asked.

"I think you are still too young!" her father said.

"Pleeeeease?" Amina begged. Her mother understood how Amina felt. "Alright, if you think you are ready. When I wake you for Suhur you can't be lazy and stay in bed. Fasting isn't easy," her mother said.

Amina was happy. She wanted to try. "Yes Mama. I will try. Thank you," she said.

Amina ran back upstairs and told Jihad that she had permission to fast. Jihad said, "You better wake up!" Amina told everyone in the house that she would be fasting. Soon it was dark and time for dinner. At dinner Amina asked, "How many hours until Suhur?"

Her grandma said, "Eight more hours." Amina couldn't wait.

Finally it was time for Suhur.
Amina's mom woke her and told
her it was time for Suhur.
Amina jumped out of bed.
Her mom said, "Wow!
You're wide awake!"

Amina and her mom
went downstairs. Her
whole family was there.
Everyone was surprised
that she wanted to fast.
They ate, prayed Fajr and
read the Quran. Afterward,
Amina went back to her
room and slept.

Later, when Amina got out of bed she brushed
her teeth, took a bath and changed her clothes.
She went downstairs and asked her mom, "What's
for breakfast?"

"Remember Amina we are fasting," her mom
replied. Amina had already forgotten. After a
few hours Amina asked her father, "Can we go
get ice cream?" But her father shook his head.

"Remember Amina we are fasting," her father
said. Amina had forgotten again. By noon Amina
really had forgotten and she ate a cookie from
the cookie jar.

"No! My fast is ruined!" Amina cried. She ran to tell her mother what happened.

"Do not worry," her mother said. "Allah will forgive you InshaAllah. If you are hungry you can fast half of the day."

But Amina was determined. "No, I don't want to fast half of the day!" she said.

When it was time for Iftar, everyone came to the dinner table. Amina's dad said a Duaa and everyone followed.

17
Tasha's
Ramadan Fast

Tasha was fasting for Ramadan, but some of her friends weren't because fasting was a challenge. When she went to school she asked her teacher if she was fasting. "Yes," her teacher said, "I'm fasting."

"But why do we fast?" Tasha asked. It was something her friends wanted to know about also.

"We fast because we want to feel what the poor feel when they are hungry. We also fast so we can learn self-control," her teacher explained to the whole class.

The class was excited because Ramadan was the best month of the year. They had a vacation, but they had a lot of homework to do anyway. Some students went traveling with their families and some students stayed at home. But it was hard to do so much homework.

The students asked the teacher if they could have less homework. The teacher said, "Okay, but if you do not finish it you are going to be in trouble."

The students were so happy and promised to finish every single thing the teacher gave them to do.

When school was out that afternoon, Tasha and her brother were the last ones to leave.

Tasha checked the clock when she got home. It was not time to break their fast yet so she went straight to her room to do her homework.

When she was finished she took a shower. Then it was time to break the fast. She put on her clothes and got ready to eat her Iftar. Then Tasha prayed Maghrib.

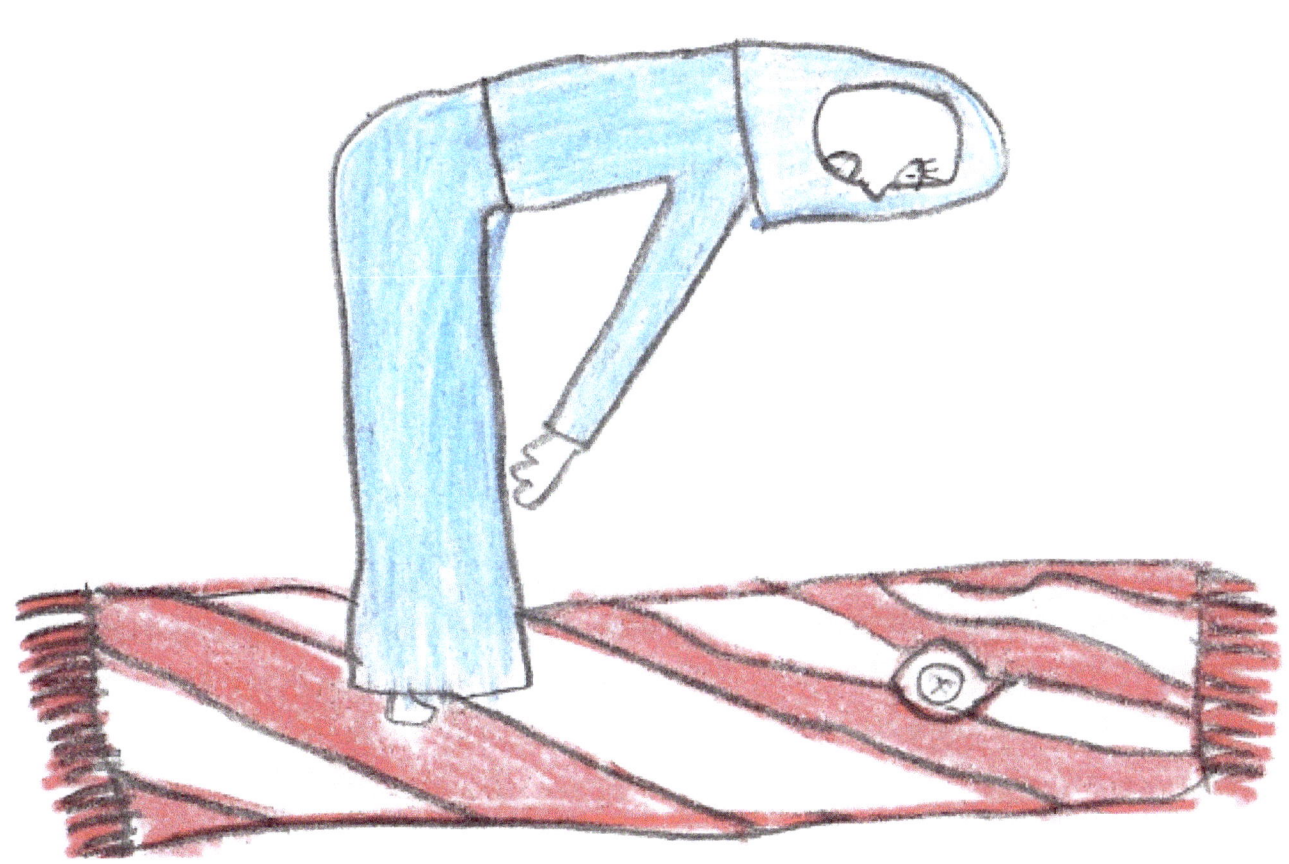

She went into the kitchen to break her fast with her family. Tasha said the Duaa before she broke her fast, and then she ate her favorite dates and some cookies.

Next, she brushed her teeth and went to her bed to go to sleep, but she couldn't sleep so she decided to read the Quran until she felt sleepy. Then she closed the Quran and then closed her eyes. Just as she was falling asleep, she thought about how she wanted to fast again tomorrow.

18
"Try to Fast Adam"

Written & Illustrated
By: Rizan Aziman
New Horizon
School LA

There was once a boy named Adam. His mom told him to fast tomorrow, and he said he would try.

When it was the next day, he forgot to fast. Now he wanted to try to fast the next day.

The next day he went to school where his friends were fasting. One of his friends asked him, "Why aren't you fasting?"

82

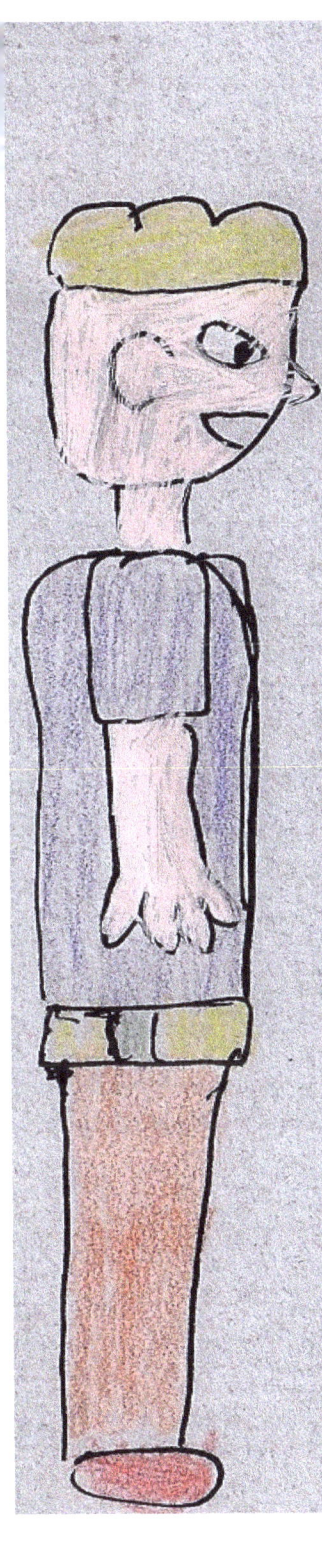

Adam ran back home upset.
When he went back home,
he did his homework.

While he was doing his
homework, his mom came
to him and said, "Why are
you acting strange today?"

Adam told her, "All my friends
are fasting and I'm not."

Then his mom told him to try to
fast tomorrow.

So next day Adam fasted all day.

He almost forgot again
and ate a cupcake but he stopped
himself just in time.

19
Ramadan

The first day of Ramadan Maryam was really happy. She woke up at Suhur time and ate. Then she slept and woke up at 7 o'clock. She thought she had to go to school, but she had a vacation. So she read the Quran. When she finished reading the Quran, she played with her friends. Then one of her friends asked Maryam, "Are you fasting?"

She said, "Yes, are you?" Her friend said yes also.

The next day was Maryam's birthday. She invited her friends to a party even though it was Ramadan.

Her friends gave her a lot of gifts. After that Maryam gave them goody bags but reminded them not to eat till Iftar time. At Iftar her mother made a lot of good food.

The next day Mayram woke up at Suhur again and ate. When she finished eating she prayed Fajr then slept again. Then she woke up in the morning and went to school.

At recess time she got hungry, but she was fasting so she did not eat. Then after four hours it was Iftar time.

20
Jamal's
First Fast

One evening Jamal was jumping around excitedly. He couldn't wait till tomorrow. It was the first day of Ramadan. He wanted to fast. He had never fasted before. After dinner Jamal ran to his room and quickly changed his clothes and went to sleep. After seven hours Jamal's alarm woke him up. It was 3:00 a.m. He ran downstairs to the dining table and found his parents already there.

After Jamal finished eating his Suhur, he ran back to his bed and slept.

That morning Jamal woke up excited.

He quickly changed into his school clothes. He already knew that he couldn't eat otherwise he would break his fast too early.

At school he felt like a man and told his friends that he was fasting.

At recess Jamal felt a little bit hungry but he didn't care because he was fasting.

At lunch Jamal felt really hungry. But instead of eating or drinking Jamal went out to play to keep food out of his mind. After lunch, Jamal went toward his class but he came across a water fountain. He took a sip and all of a sudden he remembered that he was fasting!

He felt sad and miserable. But then he remembered what his mom said, "If you break your fast too early because you forgot, just ask for Allah's forgiveness and continue fasting."

When Jamal went home his mom asked him how his fast was. Jamal told her what happened, but he wasn't sad. Tomorrow was another day!

21

<u>First Fast</u>

It was Ramadan. It was the best month of the year. All of the Muslims would fast. They would not eat from morning till night and Jamaal wanted to fast too.

The day before, Jamaal went home and asked his mom, "Can I fast this year?" "But you are only six," his mom said. "You don't have to fast." So Jamaal said, " But Muhammed gets to fast."

"Yes, but he is 10," his mom said.

"Fatima gets to fast," he said.

"Fatima is eight," she said, "and she does not fast all month."

Jamaal looked sad.

"It is hard to fast," said his mom. "You cannot eat, you cannot drink and you cannot say bad things."

"I can do it," said Jamaal. "Please let me try." "Alright," said his mom. "A full day is a long time, if you get tired you may eat."

"I will not get tired," he said. Jamaal's mom smiled and said, "I am happy you want to fast, I know Allah is happy too."

That night Jamaal told his dad, "I will fast all day. I will not get tired."

"Okay," said his dad. "You may try."

After dinner they all went to the mosque. There were many people there and they all prayed in lines.

Jamaal got tired because it was late at night. He wanted to sleep. It was hard to keep his eyes open. So Jamaal went to the back of the mosque to lie down. Soon he was asleep.

"Get up," said Jamaal's dad.

He was so tired he did not know all the people were leaving the mosque. They were all going home to sleep. Jamaal did not move. His eyes did not open. He was so tired he did not know where he was.

"Are we going home now?" Jamaal asked. His dad smiled and said, "You are not at the mosque anymore, you are in your bed!"

"Oh!" said Jamaal. He sat up and said, "Today I am fasting!"

"Yes," said his dad. "You must eat food now before the sun comes up.

Jamaal went downstairs to the table. His mom, Fatima and Muhammed were there.
It was still dark outside and after about 15 minutes the sunlight started to come out.

They all prayed and went back to bed.

After a while it was time for school. Jamaal's teacher, Miss Maryam, said, "It is Ramadan today, who is fasting?" Only one hand went up and that was Jamaal's.

Miss Maryam said that she would help him fast and at lunchtime he can rest in the classroom because he might get hungry. "But if you get tired tell me so I can give you some food," she said. "I will not get tired," said Jamaal.

The first part of the day was not hard. It went by very fast and soon it was lunchtime then it was time to go home. When he got home Jamaal prayed and read the Quran then went to sleep.

"Get up," said his dad. "It is time for Iftar." Jamaal jumped up and said, "I did it!"

The food was ready to eat now. Jamaal was very happy.

"How was your first fast?" they asked him.

Jamaal said, "I love fasting and I can do it again mom."

22
The Day Naem Learned About Patience

Written &
Illustrated By:
Sufian Hussaini
New Horizon
School LA

There was once a boy named Naem. He loved fasting because he did not like to eat or drink a lot. His mom and dad always used to tell him to eat his dinner, but he wouldn't eat. Sometimes he didn't eat lunch or dinner for seven days in a row!

Ramadan was his favorite month of the year because he did not have to eat from dawn till sunset.

But one day in Ramadan he got so hungry that he forgot he was fasting and he ate all the muffins, dates, sweets and figs his mom kept for their guests.

When his mom found out she was upset. Naem got really mad at her and reminded her that she was supposed to be patient in Ramadan.

So she apologized to him.

97

23
<u>Fatima's Mistake</u>

Written By:
Sumayya Hussaini

Illustrated By:
Hadeer Soliman
New Horizon School LA

There was once a girl named Fatima. She was 12 years old.

When she went to school no one was fasting on the first day of Ramadan and she was mad but she didn't want to force anybody to fast.

When it was lunchtime, by mistake, Fatima ate some of her friend's snack. Later she remembered that she had broken her fast so she got sad.

At home her mom asked her what happened and she told her. Then her mom got a big smile on her face.

Fatima saw her and asked,
"Why are you happy rather than sad?"

Her mom told her that Ramadan did not even start yet so she had nothing to worry about.

"No wonder no one was fasting in my school today," said Fatima.

24
Maryam's First Ramadan

In a quiet neighborhood there was a girl named Mayram. She turned six on December 16th and she decided that she should learn how to start fasting since the next day was Ramadan. When her parents agreed she got very excited. Maryam woke up early in the morning and ate until she and her parents were full. In the morning they prayed, said a Duaa and read the Quran.

She got sleepy after that and went to bed. Since it was Saturday, Maryam had nothing to do, so she decided to find something to do like paint pictures, play with puzzles, read books and watch TV. She did anything that would keep her mind off of food and water.

Maryam's father came home from a business meeting and hugged Maryam. He took a shower, broke his fast with a date and prayed. After he prayed he came out to eat with his family.

Maryam's father was so happy because Maryam helped clean the house and set the table with her mom.

While Maryam was in bed she thought of how proud her parents were of her that she finally fasted her first time and wanted to do it again. Then she smiled happily.

25
Ahmed's Very
First Fast

On the night before Ramadan, Ahmed and his family were preparing for the first fast of the month.

Ahmed asked his mom, "Will you please wake me up for Suhur?" His mom answered, "Of course, if you want."

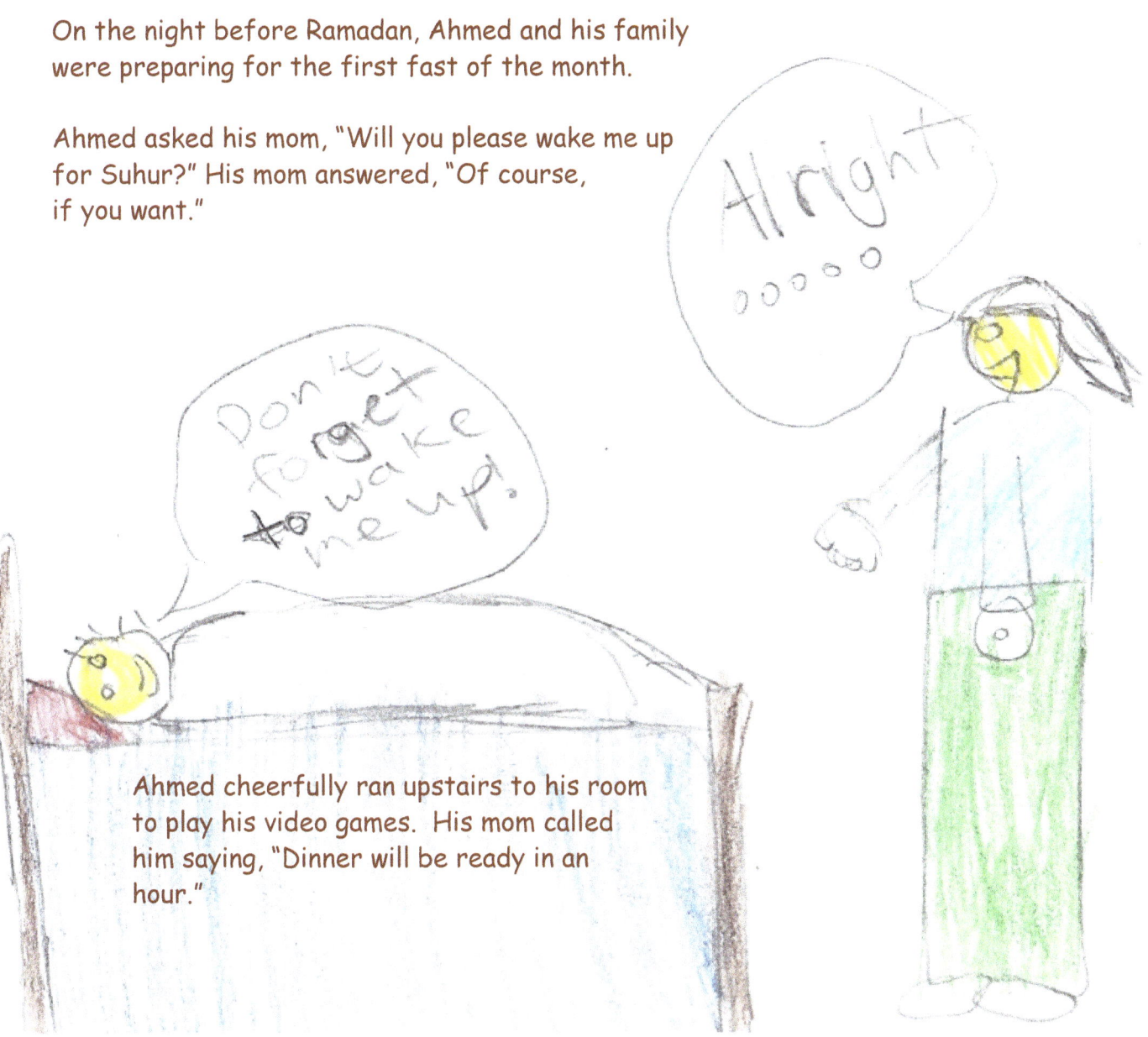

Ahmed cheerfully ran upstairs to his room to play his video games. His mom called him saying, "Dinner will be ready in an hour."

After almost an hour, Ahmed walked downstairs with his game and his trading cards in his hand. Then his twin brother followed him down the stairs. Ahmed and his brother Mahmoud are both 10 years old.

Mahmoud was also carrying his game. Their sister Aisha came down with her lap top computer. She was the oldest of the three children.

Their father came from his office to join them for dinner. They all gathered around the dinner table.

After dinner, Aisha, Mahmoud and Ahmed ate ice cream for dessert. Their parents ate chocolate pie.

After dessert the whole family said their intentions for Ramadan and then prepared for prayer.

Ahmed's dad led the prayer and then they all read Quran and prayed Taraweeh prayer. Then Ahmed and his brother and sister got ready for bedtime. They brushed their teeth, washed their faces and took a shower. Finally they were tucked in their beds and Ahmed's mother came to kiss him good night. Ahmed went to sleep quickly.

At 2:30 a.m. sharp Ahmed's mom woke him up. He got up quickly and brushed his teeth. Hurrying, he quickly wore his slippers and climbed down the stairs. He met his brother and sister and dad on the stairs. They all said their Duaa and ate a light meal of ice cream and chocolate wafers. They hurried to their rooms and went to sleep again. Then at 4:30 a.m. Ahmed and his family prayed Fajr prayer and got ready for the day.

Today Ahmed went with his dad to buy a new version of his trading cards and game. While on their way Ahmed's dad had to drop off a document to his boss. Ahmed went along. His dad's boss's wife offered Ahmed a candy bar. Ahmed was about to accept when his dad reminded him, "Do you really want to break your fast half way through the day?" So Ahmed didn't accept.

An hour before sunset Ahmed went to the kitchen clutching his stomach. His mother said, "Don't worry, it is almost time." After she put the rice on the stove Ahmed's mom left the kitchen. Then Ahmed saw a plate of cookies, and forgetting that he was fasting, he grabbed a cookie and ate it.

After tasting it he grabbed another cookie and half way through eating it he stopped and remembered! He shouted, "What have I done?" His mother came in and Ahmed explained what happened. His mother said, "It is okay since you forgot. Allah is forgiving. But if you still want to fast just continue until it is time to break the fast."

Ahmed broke his fast with juice and dates. Then after dinner the family prayed Taraweeh prayers.

26
Khadija

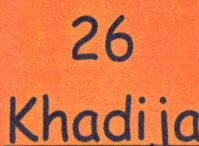

Written By:
Sumayya Hussaini

Illustrated By:
Hadeer Soliman
New Horizon School LA

The day before Ramadan a girl named Khadija was getting ready for her fast tomorrow. She was seven years old and she was very excited. She was so curious, so she kept asking her mom questions about the rules of fasting and her mom kept answering her.

Unfortunately, the next day Khadija got sick and she was sad that she might not be able to fast. But even if her mom said that she shouldn't fast in that condition, Khadija still fasted.

The next morning she woke up and got ready and she was about to eat but she stopped herself before she took a bite.

She went to school and she was the only one that was fasting. When it came time for lunch and everyone was eating, she got tempted to eat but she didn't. When her teacher asked her why she isn't eating, she said that she was fasting.

She was so happy that she told the principal and they gave her a present.

Then her dad picked her up from school and she told him all about her day. The she went home and told her mom too.

At Iftar, when they all got together, Khadija started to feel sicker. So her mom fed her quickly, gave her some medicine and put her to sleep.

The next day she woke up in the morning and she was fine so she fasted.

After the day was over her parents surprised her with nice presents. She was so happy.

Afterwards she said, "The main thing that mattered was that I made Allah happy."

27
Visitors

Written &
Illustrated By:
Rezwan Kabir
New Horizon School LA

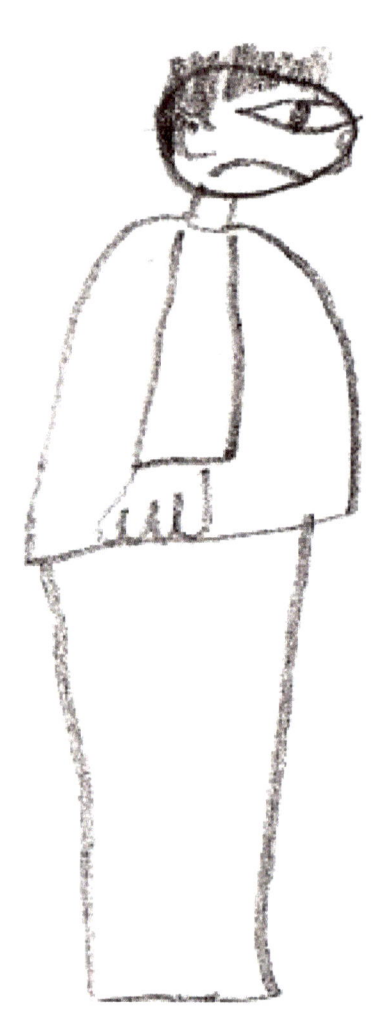

"Assalamu Alaikum," said Halib. "Waalaikum Salam," replied his aunt and cousin. Halib and his mom invited them to their house for Iftar. His mom and aunt talked a little while Habib and his cousin, Thurman, played before eating.

When it was time to eat everyone gathered and sat around the table. Then everyone said, "Bismillah" and started to eat. Halib and Thurman started eating fast because they wanted to play, but their moms got angry.

Halib and Thurman both wanted
to play with the computer game
first. They had a contest
to decide who would go first.

Since Halib won the contest
Thurman got upset. Then
Halib said, "You could go first
because you are our guest."

When it came time for
them to leave, they
became sad. Then
Thurman's mom said,
"We can come back
 next week."

Then they were happy
again. They both said
bye to each other.

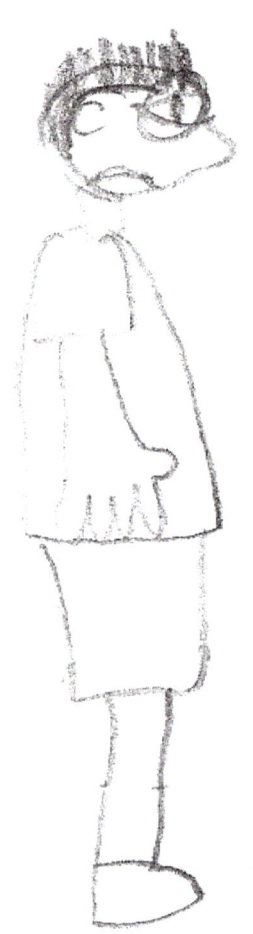

28
Me and My
Friend Lisa

Written &
Illustrated By:
Hirra Shahid
New Horizon School LA

One day in Ramadan, my Christian friend Lisa and I went to a mosque. When we got there Lisa was about to go in with her shoes on. I told her to stop and she said, "Why?"

I told her that in a mosque we are not allowed to wear our shoes because they are dirty and a mosque is a place of worship, therefore we have to take our shoes off and say a Duaa.

"What Duaa should we say?" asked Lisa. I told her to repeat after me and she did.

We sat in a women's section. Lisa asked me, "Why are we sitting behind the men? In our church we sit on benches together."

I told her that in Islam we pray while sitting on the floor and men and women are not allowed to pray together in the same row.

Also, women have to cover their head with Hijab so their hair cannot be seen. Lisa was interested in Islam, so I told her that to be a Muslim one has to believe in five things: Belief in one God and that Prophet Muhammad (peace be upon him) is the last prophet, pray five times a day, fast in Ramadan, pay Zakat charity and perform Hajj.

I told Lisa that we couldn't talk while the Imam is speaking and she asked, "Why?"

After the prayers Lisa asked me to tell her more about Islam.

On our way back home, we stopped at the library and checked out a few books about Islam for her to read.

29
<u>The Fast</u>

Written & Illustrated By:
Rezwan Kabir
New Horizon School LA

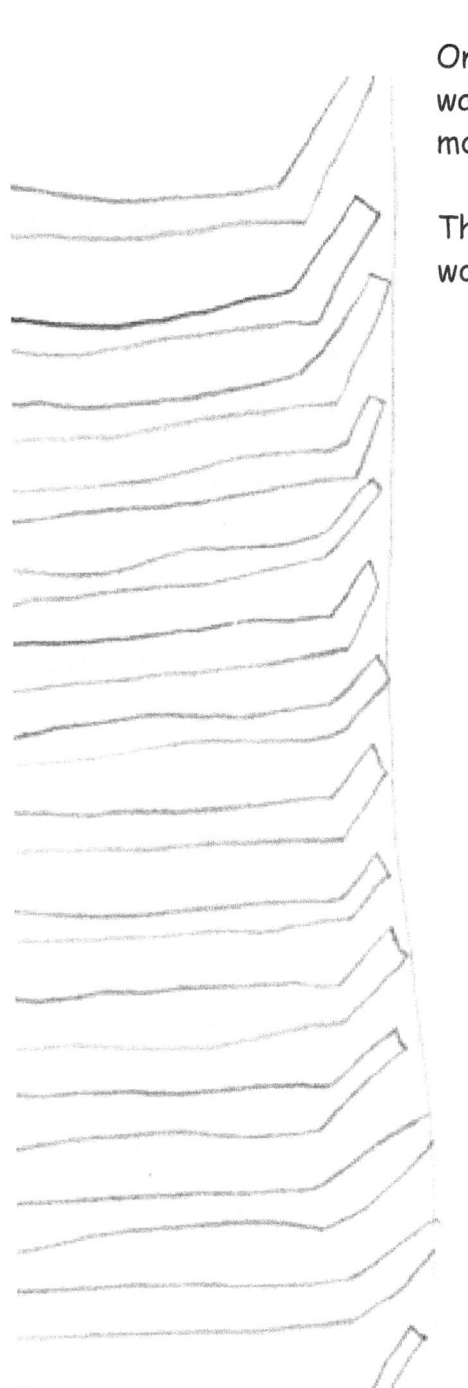

Once there was a boy named Qadir who lived in New York. It was the end of Ramadan and he had to fast one more day. His mom came and said, "Qadir quickly get ready."

They were going to his sister's wedding in California. So Qadir wore his watch and left quickly.

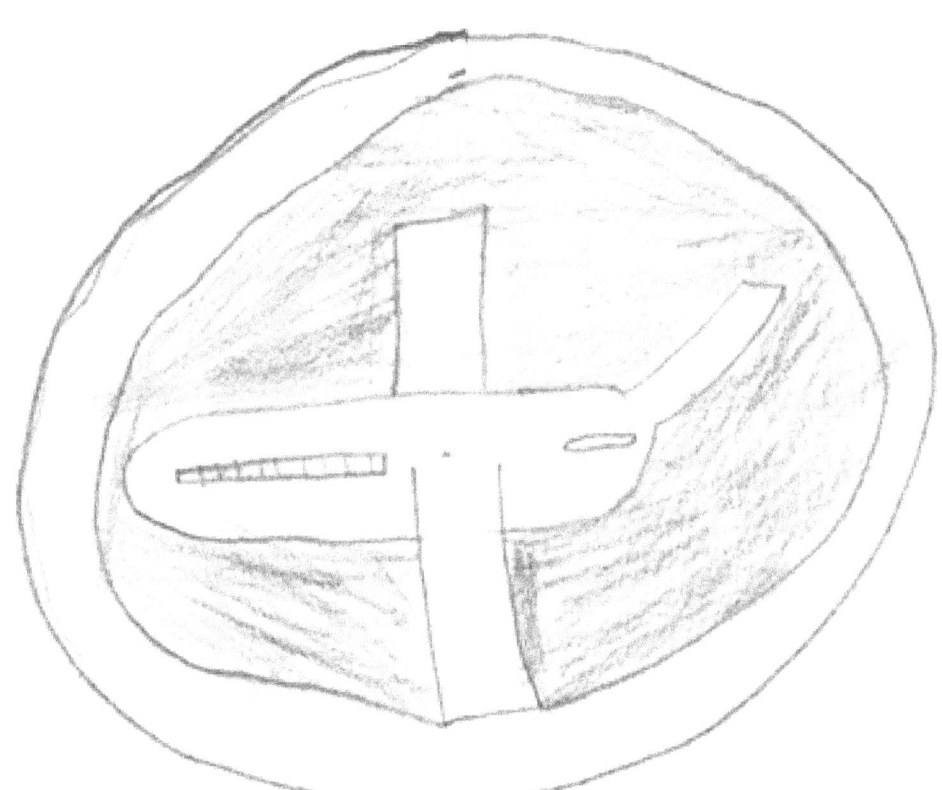

When they got there, Qadir looked at his watch and saw that is said 9:00 p.m. He went to his aunt's house and went straight to bed. He looked out the window though and said to himself, "It sure looks lighter than 9:00 p.m."

The next morning, he woke up at 5:15 a.m according to his watch. "Time for Suhur," he told himself. But when he got up, everybody was asleep and there was no food on the table.

He asked his mom what was happening, and she told him that New York time is three hours faster!

It was only 2:15 a.m. That day was the last day of Ramadan, and even though he got confused for a little he was proud to have fasted all 30 days.

30
Adel and Fatima Learn How to Fast

Written &
Illustrated By:
Hirra Shahid
New Horizon School
LA

A few days ago Uncle Yahya arrived to visit for a few days.

"Ramadan is about to begin and I would like to tell you about it," said Uncle Yahya to Adel and Fatima. "Tell us!" they yelled. "Gladly," he said.

"As soon as Ramadan begins, all Muslims around the world start fasting," he said.

"What is fasting?" asked Adel.

"Fasting means not eating or drinking from dawn to sunset for the sake of Allah," he said.

"Nothing at all?" exclaimed Fatima.

"Nothing at all!" said Uncle Yahya.

"But we may have a meal before starting called Suhur."

Uncle Yahya left and Ramadan began. Adel and Fatima noticed that their parents woke up earlier than usual, and heard them going to the kitchen. They were eating the meal called Suhur. So Adel and Fatima decided to join them. "We want to have Suhur with you," they said. After eating Suhur and praying Fajr, they went to bed to sleep.

A while later, Adel and Fatima had to go to school. But this time there was no breakfast or lunch. As evening approached, their mother and father put some food on the table. They sat down and began to eat.   At night Adel and Fatima told their father to wake them up for Suhur. So the next morning their mom woke them up and they had Suhur with their parents.

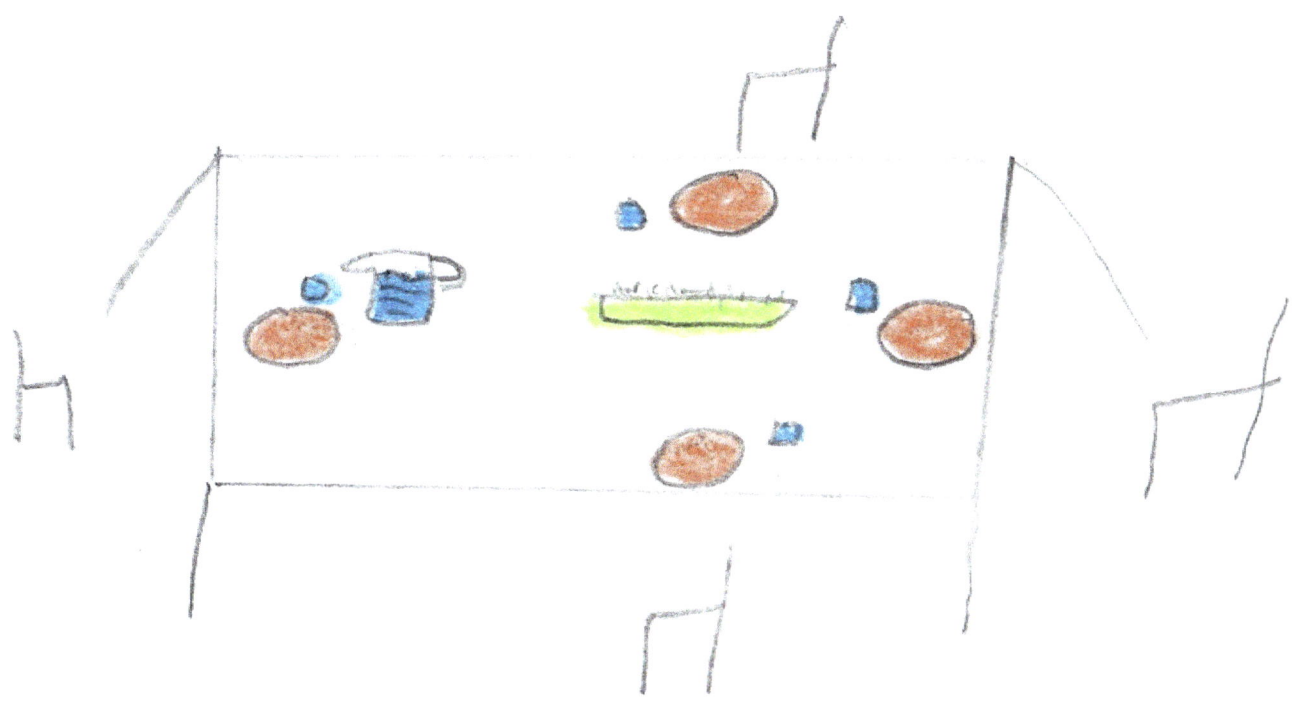

The End

Additional Thanks:

Lore Kebir

Virginia Bergquist

Marya Bangee

Some of the young writers now...

Rezwan Kabir was a Civil Engineering student at the University of California, Irvine. He was an active member of and helps coordinate events for the Campuswide Honors Student Council and the Muslim student organization. He plans on going on to graduate school to pursue a Master's in Structural Engineering. In his free time, he enjoys watching movies, playing videogames, and hanging out with his friends. He considers Islam to be a fundamental part of his life as he continues his ongoing goal to learn about Islam and better himself as a Muslim.

Hirra Shahid currently lives in Los Angeles, CA. She studied economics at the University of Southern California. Hirra plans to attend business school in the future. In her free time, she enjoys reading and traveling.

Sufian Hussaini was a student at the University of California, Los Angeles. He was a History major with an Accounting minor. He aspires to be an investment banker and an exemplary Muslim.

Some of the young writers now...

Hadeer Soliman was a senior Public Health Science and Spanish double major at the University of California, Irvine. She was an active member of the Muslim student organization and a member of the Campuswide Honors Program. She plans to go to graduate school to eventually be able to benefit the community through health communication and education. She still loves writing in her free time and is an active member of the Muslim community in Southern California.

Hakim Kebir attended the University of California, Irvine. He was a Biology major student and enjoys basketball and volunteering in his free time. He aspires to be a doctor and hopes to be able to benefit Muslim youth with his work.

Siraj Soliman attended the University of California, Riverside. He was a Business Administration major and is interested in Accounting. He is a New Horizon School, Los Angeles alumni, he is a member of the Muslim community in Southern California and enjoys spending time with his friends and hopes to benefit the Muslim community.

www.ingramcontent.com/pod-product-compliance
Lightning Source LLC
Chambersburg PA
CBHW041639010726

47507CB00011B/410